HOLOCAUST

The Story of a Survivor

Dee Phillips

READZONE

First published in this edition 2013

ReadZone Books Limited
50 Godfrey Avenue
Twickenham
TW2 7PF
UK

Every attempt has been made by the Publisher to secure appropriate permissions for material reproduced in this book. If there has been any oversight we will be happy to rectify the situation in future editions or reprints. Written submissions should be made to the Publishers.

British Library Cataloguing in Publication Data (CIP) is available for this title.

ISBN 978-1-78322-007-6

Printed in China

Developed and Created by Ruby Tuesday Books Ltd
Project Director – Ruth Owen
Designer – Elaine Wilkinson

Images are in the public domain or courtesy of Shutterstock.

Acknowledgements
With thanks to Lorraine Petersen, Chief Executive of NASEN,
for her help in the development and creation of these books

Visit our website: www.readzonebooks.com

They took my clothes.
They shaved my head.
I was given a prisoner number.
I was no longer a human.

HOLOCAUST

The Story of a Survivor

In 1939, Germany was at war with
Britain and many other countries.
Germany's leader was called Adolf Hitler.
Hitler led a group called the Nazis.

The Nazis hated the Jews.
They bullied the Jews.
They made their lives hell.

The Nazis sent the Jews to
concentration camps.

Six million Jews were killed in
these camps.

This time is known as
THE HOLOCAUST

Tonight there is a full moon.
I look up and think of Jacob.

I met Jacob in 1939.
He came to teach my little brother, David.
I would take Jacob coffee.
He would smile at me.
I would smile back.

One evening we went for a walk.
There was a beautiful full moon.
We were so happy.
But life was changing in Poland.

At night my father's friends came.
I would take them coffee.
They talked about the war.
They talked about Hitler
and the Nazis.
They talked about camps where
Jews were slaves.

They said, "It's a bad time to be a Jew."

One day Jacob and I were
in the town square.
A boy spat at Jacob.

The boy said,

"DIRTY JEWS."

I was afraid.

Then the Germans invaded Poland.
Now the Nazis were in charge.
Nazi soldiers came for us.
BANG! BANG! On the door.

"ALL JEWS OUTSIDE NOW!"

We walked to the town square.
I held my little brother's hand.

I saw Jacob.
I said, "I'm afraid.
What if we are split up?"

Jacob said, "I will find you, Sarah.
When there is a full moon,
think of me. I will be thinking
of you."

A soldier shouted at me, "Go left."
To my mother and brother, "Go left."
To my father and Jacob, "Go right."

Jacob shouted, "I will find you!"

David 1939

Mother and Father 1934

The soldiers put us on a train.
The train took us to a camp.

A soldier shouted at me, "Go left."
To my mother and brother, "Go right."
I tried to go right, too.
But the soldiers stopped me.

I shouted, "I will find you!"

Tonight there is a full moon.
I look up and think of my family.
I think of Jacob.
It has been 70 years.
But I will never forget.

They took my clothes.
They shaved my head.
I was given a
prisoner number.

I WAS NO LONGER A HUMAN.

I waited in line for food.
A bowl of brown, smelly water.
A piece of dry bread.
I couldn't eat it.

I DIDN'T KNOW ABOUT HUNGER THEN.

I slept on a wooden bunk.
No blanket. No pillow.

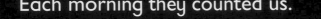
Each morning they counted us.

WE STOOD IN THE ICY RAIN...

...IN THE COLD SNOW...

...IN THE HOT SUN.

Some women could not go on.

Each day we went to work.
Digging the frozen ground.
Carrying rocks.

I waited for each full moon.
I would think of Jacob.

"I will find you...."

I had to keep going.

Weeks and months passed by.
Then years.

We were starving.
My body turned to bones.

MANY WOMEN DIED.

Their bodies were burned.
Women just like me – turned to smoke.

I became ill.

I lay on my bunk.

The guards would shoot me now.

I saw a full moon rising. I said,

"I'm sorry Jacob,
but I can't go on."

I was ready to die.

I will never forget that next morning.
The guards didn't come.
The American soldiers came.

They told us, "The war is over.
You are free."

I had survived.

The Americans took us to another camp.
There was food and medicine.
There were thousands of men and
women just like me.
I had to find my family.
I had to find Jacob.

David 1939

Mother and Father 1934

Every day I looked at lists of names.
I wrote letters.
But I never found my family.
They were all killed.
Killed in the camps.
Killed in the gas chambers.
I kept looking for Jacob.
Was he looking for me?

Tonight there is a full moon.
I look up at the moon.
It has been 70 years.
But I will never forget.

My husband touches my arm.
He says, "I have been looking for you.
Come inside. It's late."

I smile and say, "My Jacob. Always
looking for me."

HOLOCAUST:

Behind the Story

In the 1930s, Germany was led by the Nazis. The Nazis needed someone to blame for Germany's problems. One of the groups they picked on was the Jews. Many Jews were beaten, and their homes and businesses destroyed.

During the Second World War, the Nazis invaded other countries, such as Poland. In those countries, they also singled out certain groups as their enemies. Many people were sent to concentration camps and forced to work as slaves. Most of these people were Jews.

Some concentration camps were called death camps. In these camps, people were shot or sent to buildings known as gas chambers.

These women
were freed from the
Bergen-Belsen concentration camp
in Germany. They are carrying loaves of bread.

Once people were inside a gas chamber, the
Nazis released poisonous gas into the building.
Hundreds of people were killed at a time.
By the end of the war, millions of people had
been murdered by the Nazis.

After the Holocaust

When the war ended, soldiers from America,
Britain and other countries freed the people
held in concentration camps.

New camps were set up where survivors could
live while they recovered.

Jewish groups tried to reunite families.
They made lists of the names of survivors
and where those people were living. The lists
were then sent to all the different camps.

HOLOCAUST— What's next?

A FULL MOON
ON YOUR OWN

When they are apart, Sarah and Jacob watch for a full moon as a way to stay connected.

Imagine you are about to be separated from someone you love. You cannot text, phone, or contact that person online. Think of some ways to stay connected.

- Wear friendship bracelets.
- Watch our favourite TV show at the same time each week.

FACES AND FEELINGS
ON YOUR OWN

The sadness I felt when Grandpa died.

Look at how the colours black, grey and blue are used in the book to show the horror of Sarah's time in the concentration camp.

Think of a time when you felt great pain, sadness, fear or happiness. Then take a photograph of your face and using paints or a computer programme, add colours or patterns to your face that show your feelings during that time.

BOOK TALK
IN A GROUP

Sarah and Jacob are characters in a story. Their story, however, is based on what happened to millions of real people because of racism and prejudice. Discuss with your group how the story and the facts you've learned about the Holocaust make you feel. Think about:

- How does it feel to be hated because of your race?

- What did it feel like to be the only person in a family to survive the Holocaust?

I WILL FIND YOU!
WITH A PARTNER / IN A GROUP

Imagine that after the war, Sarah is living at a camp for survivors. One day, a young man arrives at the camp. It is Jacob! He has been searching for her.

With a partner, role-play the couple's meeting.

- What would they say?

- How would they feel?

- How would they have changed?

Titles in the
Yesterday's Voices
series

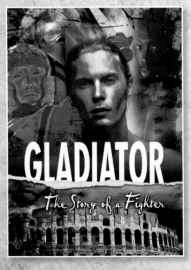

I waited deep below the arena.
Then it was my turn to fight.
Kill or be killed!

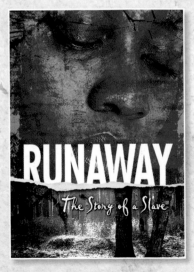

I cannot live as a slave
any longer. Tonight, I will
escape and never go back.